Helping Out

At the Zoo

Judith Heneghan

WAYLAND

First published in 2011 by Wayland

Copyright © Wayland 2011

Wayland
Hachette Children's Books
338 Euston Road
London NW1 3BH

Wayland Australia
Level 17/207 Kent Street
Sydney, NSW 2000

Editor: Louise John
Designer: Robert Walster, Big Blu Design

British Library Cataloguing in Publication Data

Anderson, Judith, 1965-
   At the zoo. -- (Helping out)
   1. Zoos--Juvenile literature. 2. Zoo animals--Juvenile
   literature. 3. Zoo keepers--Juvenile literature.
   I. Title II. Series
   590.7'3-dc22

ISBN-13: 9780750264907

Printed in China
Wayland is a division of Hachette Children's Books,
an Hachette UK company. www.hachette.co.uk

Picture acknowledgements
All photography by Adam Lawrence

With special thanks to all the staff at Beale Park.

Disclaimer
The website addresses (URLs) included in this book
were valid at the time of going to press. However,
because of the nature of the Internet, it is possible that
some addresses may have changed, or sites may have
changed or closed down since publication. While the
author and Publisher regret any inconvenience this
may cause the readers, no responsibility for any such
changes can be accepted by either the author or the
Publisher.

Contents

Meeting the keepers 4

Looking around 6

Important jobs 8

Preparing the food 10

Meeting the lemurs 12

Feeding the lemurs 14

Cleaning and sweeping 16

Lemur play 18

Lemur babies 20

A brilliant day 22

Glossary 24

Index 24

Meeting the keepers

Joe is spending the day at a zoo. He is going to help look after the lemurs. People who look after animals are called **keepers**. Dave, the Head Keeper, meets Joe at the front gate.

Dave is in charge of caring for all the animals.

Joe's diary

I can't wait to see the lemurs! I hope I'll be allowed to get close to them.

Joe puts on a special shirt to show that he is a keeper for the day.

There are five keepers at the zoo and they all have different jobs. Mark looks after the ring-tailed lemurs. Joe is going to help him today.

Looking around

First Mark shows Joe around the zoo. They walk past the train and the pond where the waterfowl live. They stop to give some treats to the meerkats. Some goats are enjoying the sunshine nearby.

That's AMAZING!

Toby is an Arapawa Goat. He is thought to be a relative of the two goats that Captain Cook first brought to the UK from New Zealand.

Mark says the meerkats are very popular with visitors.

Not all of the animals stay in **enclosures**. The peafowl wander freely in the grounds. They don't escape because they are only able to fly short distances.

The peacocks only open their tail feathers when they want to impress the peahens!

Important jobs

The keepers do lots of important jobs around the zoo. They keep the animals' enclosures clean and wash the windows of their sleeping areas. They prepare their food and change their bedding.

Joe's diary

Mark showed me the bug hotel. It provides shelter for lots of insects. I'm going to make one in my garden at home!

When the windows are clean, visitors can see into the enclosures and the animals can look out!

Some keepers also help to conserve wildlife. They look after a wildflower meadow, which attracts insects, and build nesting boxes for birds, which they put up around the zoo.

This bug hotel was made by some of the keepers.

Preparing the food

Now it is time to look after the lemurs. Mark takes Joe to the kitchen, where the keepers prepare the animals' food. They chop up some apples, bananas and oranges.

Joe puts the fruit into bowls for the lemurs.

They are almost ready to go to the lemurs' enclosure when Mark remembers something else - grapes! 'We can't forget these!' he says. 'Grapes are the lemurs' favourite treats!'

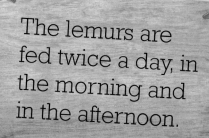

The lemurs are fed twice a day, in the morning and in the afternoon.

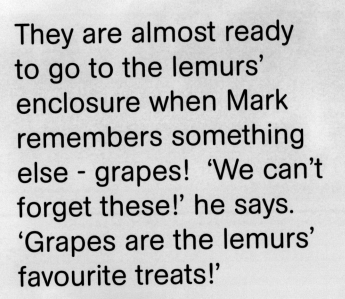

Meeting the lemurs

The lemurs are inside their hut when Joe and Mark arrive. 'They are very friendly,' says Mark. 'Show them the treats.'

Soon the lemurs come outside. There are eight of them – five males and three females.

Joe's diary

The lemurs are so friendly. One even sat on my lap! When I offered them the grapes, they took them from my hand!

Lemurs live in groups called **troops**.

Mark tells Joe that lemurs come from an island called Madagascar, in the Indian Ocean. There are over 70 different types of lemur. These ones are called ring-tailed lemurs.

Lemurs spend a lot of time in trees. Their long tails help them to **balance**.

Feeding the lemurs

When all the lemurs have met Joe, it is time to give them their meal. Mark and Joe hold the bowls and the lemurs pick up the fruit in their hands.

These lemurs eat fruit and vegetables, but in the wild they sometimes eat insects and tree bark.

Lemurs have four fingers and a thumb, just like we have. Joe notices that they also have a small lump on the inside of their arms.

'That's a **scent gland**,' says Mark. 'They rub it against branches.'

The scent gland leaves a scent for other lemurs to recognise.

That's AMAZING!

Sometimes the males have a stink fight. They rub their scent on their tails and wave them at their rivals to see who's the stinkiest!

Cleaning and sweeping

While the lemurs are outside, Mark and Joe go into their hut. It is time to do some cleaning! Mark washes the sleeping platforms while Joe sweeps out the dirty wood shavings. Then they sprinkle some fresh shavings on the floor.

Joe's diary

The lemurs are quite noisy! They make lots of clicks and grunts. Mark says this is how they 'talk' to each other.

A keeper's job involves lots of cleaning.

The lemurs need fresh drinking water every day.

Joe also cleans the pond and fills it with fresh water from the tap.
The lemurs use this for drinking water as well as for playing.

Lemur play

Lemurs are **sociable** animals. They like being in a troop and they like to play. The keepers need to make sure they have lots of interesting things to explore in their enclosure.

That's AMAZING!

Females are dominant in lemur troops. This means they are in charge. They get to choose the best food and the warmest place to sleep.

Mark and Joe hang up a new toy for the lemurs to play with.

Rosie and Sam are
the oldest lemurs
in the troop.

Sam and Rosie
are both over
20 years old.
Rosie is the most
important lemur in
the troop and she
gets to boss the
others around!

Lemur babies

Rosie gave birth to lemur **triplets** nearly a year ago, and they are now almost adult-sized. It is quite unusual for lemurs to have triplets. Mark says they usually have just one or two babies.

Lulu, middle, likes nothing more than playing with her brother and sister.

Lemurs love lying back and enjoying the sunshine.

Ring-tailed lemurs are **endangered** animals. They are under **threat** in the wild. This is because the forests they live in are being **destroyed**. However, there are plenty of lemurs in zoos around the world.

A brilliant day

Now it's time for Joe to go home. He says goodbye to the lemurs and he and Mark walk back past the lake. The other keepers are still busy with their work.

Joe's diary

I can't believe I got to name one of the lemurs! They are my favourite animals. I'd really like to be a zookeeper one day.

Joe locks the door to the lemur enclosure, so that the lemurs do not escape.

'Thank you,' says Joe. 'I've had a brilliant day.' 'You've been a big help,' says Mark. 'Come and see us again soon!'

Joe stops by the lake to give the bar-headed ducks a treat.

Glossary

Balance to stay upright

Destroyed ruined

Enclosures an area where animals are kept with a fence or wall around it so that they cannot escape

Endangered when an animal species is at danger of becoming extinct

Keepers the people who look after the animals

Scent gland a small patch of skin that produces a smell when rubbed

Sociable friendly

Triplets three babies born to one mother at the same time

Troop a small group of animals

Threat in danger of disappearing from the wild

Index

animals 4, 8, 10

babies 20

bar-headed ducks 23

bug hotel 8, 9

cleaning 16

endangered 21

food 8, 10

fruit 11, 14

goats 6

keepers 4, 5, 8, 9, 11, 16, 22

Madagascar 13

meercats 6

peafowl 7

play 18

scent gland 15

tails 13, 15

talk 16

troops 12, 18, 19

water 17

waterfowl 6

wildlife 9

Helping Out

Contents of titles in the series:

FARM

An early start
Cleaning the cow barn
Milking time
Feeding the calves
Cleaning the equipment
Feeding the cows
Chewing the cud
A visit from the vet
More milking
Time to go home

AQUARIUM

Visiting the aquarium
Looking in the tanks
Food preparation
Feeding the rays
Water samples
The rainforest area
Feeding the sharks
Coral reef zone
Feeding the turtles
Time to go home

ZOO

Meeting the keepers
Looking around
Important jobs
Preparing the food
Meeting the lemurs
Feeding the lemurs
Cleaning and sweeping
Lemur play
Lemur babies
A brilliant day

DOG RESCUE CENTRE

Saying hello
Meeting the dogs
A new arrival
Time for a walk
Daily chores
Feeding the puppies
Talking to the vet nurse
Training fun
Finding a home
Time to say goodbye

WAYLAND